TRUE SURVIVAL GRAPHICS

LOST in the JUNGLE

by Steve Foxe
illustrated by Daniele Dickmann

a Capstone company — publishers for children

Raintree is an imprint of Capstone Global Library Limited, a company incorporated in England and Wales having its registered office at 264 Banbury Road, Oxford, OX2 7DY – Registered company number: 6695582

www.raintree.co.uk
myorders@raintree.co.uk

Copyright © 2025 Capstone Global Library Limited
The moral rights of the proprietor have been asserted.

All rights reserved. No part of this publication may be reproduced in any form or by any means (including photocopying or storing it in any medium by electronic means and whether or not transiently or incidentally to some other use of this publication) without the written permission of the copyright owner, except in accordance with the provisions of the Copyright, Designs and Patents Act 1988 or under the terms of a licence issued by the Copyright Licensing Agency, 5th Floor, Shackleton House, 4 Battle Bridge Lane, London SE1 2HX (www.cla.co.uk). Applications for the copyright owner's written permission should be addressed to the publisher.

Editorial credits
Edited by Christopher Harbo
Designed by Tracy Davies
Production by Katy LaVigne
Printed and bound in India

978 1 3982 5668 2

British Library Cataloguing in Publication Data
A full catalogue record for this book is available from the British Library.

All the internet addresses (URLs) given in this book were valid at the time of going to press. However, due to the dynamic nature of the internet, some addresses may have changed, or sites may have changed or ceased to exist since publication. While the author and publisher regret any inconvenience this may cause readers, no responsibility for any such changes can be accepted by either the author or the publisher.

CONTENTS

Introduction
PERIL IN THE JUNGLE 4

Chapter 1
FREEFALL OVER THE RAINFOREST 6

Chapter 2
SCORCHED AND ALONE 18

Chapter 3
THE NEVER-ENDING JUNGLE 30

MORE ABOUT THESE TALES OF SURVIVAL 44
GLOSSARY 46
FIND OUT MORE 47
ABOUT THE AUTHOR 48
ABOUT THE ILLUSTRATOR 48

INTRODUCTION
PERIL IN THE JUNGLE

Jungles are home to many of the world's plants and animals.

They are key to life on Earth and full of wonder.

But they also hold many dangers.

We put ourselves at risk each time we enter untamed jungles.

Risks we might never expect.

Out in the wild, humans aren't always at the top of the food chain.

And as the following stories show, deep in the jungle, survival is *never* certain.

They were going to a jungle research station that Juliane's parents had built.

Suddenly . . .

KRAKABOOM!

As the plane fell, it began to break apart.

SHKREEEEEK!

Early the next morning...

I hear voices -- outside!

The local fishermen were shocked. Luckily, Juliane could speak Spanish.

"I was on a plane that crashed!"

The fishermen took Juliane to the local village. She was then airlifted to a hospital.

After she recovered, she helped find the bodies of those who died on the flight.

Of the 92 people onboard, Juliane was the only survivor.

But they got into an argument.

"Come on! Where are you going?"

"Leave me alone! I need to think."

He makes me so angry sometimes!

Shannon stomped away to clear her head.

It wasn't long before Shannon was surrounded by dense jungle.

Heath! Where are you?!

This isn't right. I should have hit the path again by now.

Meanwhile, back at the beach...

"Shannon! Where are you!?"

Failing to find her, Heath called the police.

"We're baffled. Are you sure she isn't pulling some sort of prank?"

"She's got three kids at home. She'd never do that!"

But when she failed to show up anywhere, search parties formed.

She spent a whole day climbing a nearby mountain, but that took her further from rescue.

To survive, she drank water from streams.

And she ate whatever she could find.

Yuck!

All along, Shannon avoided large bodies of water for fear of crocodiles.

"This sunburn is driving me nuts."

But after many days in the sun, her skin had blistered terribly.

"Ah, cool water."

"Finally, a little bit of relief from the itching."

Shannon was stuck on the rock.

Three days later . . .

The croc's finally gone! I have to make a run for it!

Finally, 17 days after disappearing, Shannon walked out of the jungle.

She wore a plastic bag she had found in the forest to replace her shredded clothing.

She had lost nearly 18 kilograms. And her sunburn was one of the worst doctors had ever seen.

My kids . . . I just want to see my kids.

But, somehow, Shannon had found the will to survive.

While the job was legal, the mining operation was not.

It destroyed the forest's trees and dumped toxic waste into the water.

But the pandemic had shut down Antonio's regular jobs.

He really needed the work.

"I've got to get out before the plane explodes!"

FWOOSH!

Others were large!

I can't stay near water. The risk of jaguars or anacondas is too high.

MORE ABOUT THESE TALES of SURVIVAL

The plane Juliane and Maria Koepcke flew in was a Lockheed L-188 Electra. That model had a terrible reputation. Of the 170 built, at least 58 crashed or had in-flight mechanical problems.

Juliane (Koepcke) Diller grew up to be a respected bat researcher. She still regularly flies across Peru to the research station founded by her parents.

At first, some people doubted Shannon Leah Fraser's survival story, especially since she reappeared so close to where she had disappeared. But her severe sunburn and her loss of nearly 18 kilograms helped to convince them.

Australia is home to some of the world's most venomous animals. These include the taipan snake, Sydney funnel-web spider and stonefish. But human deaths by these animals are rare.

Antonio Sena's family received several fake calls reporting he had been found. When the nut scavengers called, Antonio's family asked for proof no one could learn from news reports. They asked for the name of Antonio's brother's dog, which was Gancho.

The Amazon rainforest is the largest jungle in the world. It spreads across nine countries and contains one out of every 10 known animal species on the planet.

GLOSSARY

anaconda very long snake that wraps itself tightly around its prey to kill it

collarbone bone that is part of a person's shoulder

engagement agreement to get married

fiancé person who is engaged to be married to another person

food chain series of organisms in which each one in the series eats another one in turn

infection disease caused by germs

maggot larva of certain flies

mining digging up minerals that are underground

pandemic disease that spreads over a wide area and affects many people

piranha flesh-eating fish with very sharp teeth

reputation someone or something's worth or character, as judged by others

venomous having or producing a poison called venom

FIND OUT MORE

natgeokids.com/uk/discover/geography/physical-geography/amazon-facts
Learn some amazing Amazon facts with National Geographic Kids.

planbee.com/blogs/news/rainforest-facts-for-ks2-children-and-teachers
Discover more rainforest facts on this website.

www.wwf.org.uk/learn/love-nature/jungles
The World Wildlife Fund website has lots of information about jungles.

BOOKS IN THE SERIES

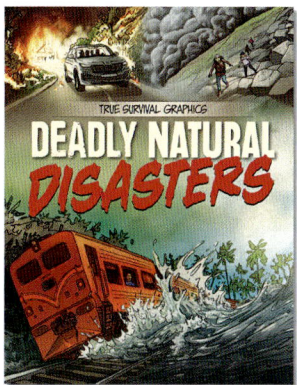
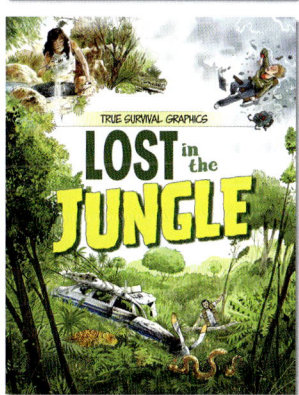
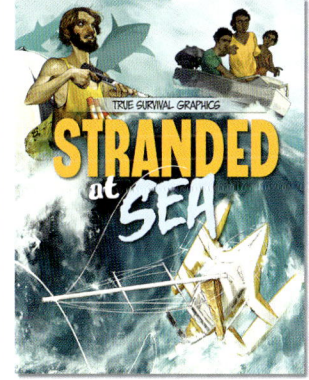

ABOUT THE AUTHOR

photo by Juni Salgado

Steve Foxe is the Eisner and Ringo Award-nominated author of more than 75 comics and children's books, including *X-Men '92: House of XCII*, *Rainbow Bridge*, *Adventure Kingdom* and the Spider-Ham series from Scholastic. He has written for properties like Pokémon, Mario, LEGO City, Batman, Justice League, Baby Shark and many more. He lives somewhere cold with his partner and dog. He once got lost in the park over the road from his house.

ABOUT THE ILLUSTRATOR

photo by Daniele Dickmann

Daniele Dickmann is a freelance artist born and raised in Rome, Italy. He graduated from the IED (Europe Institute of Design), where he's now a professor. His career began as a visual and storyboard artist for advertising companies and film productions. Daniele has since gone on to work for Usborne Publishing and many other publishing houses, illustrating historical series and fiction tales for young readers.